WATER TO SUSTAIN THE SPIRIT

poems by

John Holbrook

Finishing Line Press
Georgetown, Kentucky

WATER TO SUSTAIN
THE SPIRIT

Copyright © 2025 by John Holbrook
ISBN 979-8-89990-130-0 First Edition
All rights reserved under International and Pan-American Copyright Conventions. No part of this book may be reproduced in any manner whatsoever without written permission from the publisher, except in the case of brief quotations embodied in critical articles and reviews.

ACKNOWLEDGMENTS

Arcade: The Devil as a Second Grader
Big Sky Journal: Gone Fishin'
Blue Collar Review: Columbus, Georgia, 1959
Colorado State Review: A Cult of Salt; the Request
Country Mouse (Ezine): Archetypes; The Request
The Dance (Pudding House Chapbook Series), A Cult of Salt; Archetypes; The Dance; The Devil as a Second Grader; Gallery; Horse in the Barn, Cat in the Loft, Puddles on the Floor, Bard at his Bath
Illness and Grace/ Terror and Transformation: An Anthology: Envision
Intro #2: The Dance
Missoula Independent: Land Developers Walking into a Field; Outside Detroit, Deep in the 'Burbs; Sestina Poletti
Mississippi Review: Lines from My Pencil
New Collage: Words I like to Hear
Northern Journeys: Water to Sustain the Spirit
Pinyon: Finding Some Traction
Rain City Review: Land Developers Walking into a Field
The South Carolina Review: Sea Gull
The Talking River Review: Outside Detroit, Deep in the 'Burbs

Publisher: Leah Huete de Maines
Editor: Christen Kincaid
Cover Art: John Holbrook
Author Photo: Judith M. Holbrook
Cover Design: Elizabeth Maines McCleavy

Order online: www.finishinglinepress.com
also available on amazon.com

Author inquiries and mail orders:
Finishing Line Press
PO Box 1626
Georgetown, Kentucky 40324
USA

Contents

I

Portrait 1
Mastectomy, the Moon 2
Envision 3
Letter Back to Michigan 5

II

Archetypes 11
The Devil as a Second Grader 12
The Request 13
Sea Gull 14
Horse in the Barn, Cat in the Loft, Puddles on the Floor,
    Bard at His Bath 15
The Dance 16
Gallery 17
Ramblin' on the Way to Wallace, Idaho 19
A Cult of Salt 21
Lines from My Pencil 22
Salt Against Your Name 23
Words I Like to Hear 24
Sestina Poletti 25

III

Pastoral On a Cork Clipboard 29
Land Developers Walking into a Field 30
Outside Detroit, Deep in the 'Burbs 32
Columbus, Georgia, 1959 34
Finding Some Traction 36
Surviving Big-Boned Domestic Challenges in the Wilderness 37
Jim and the Three Bears 43
Water to Sustain the Spirit 45

IV

Jasper in Sunshine 49

I

PORTRAIT

You are gone and I am looking
at the last photo I have of you.
Of all your recent photos
this one unquestionably is the best.

Despite angina,
there is regard in your face
reaching beyond
your years of suffering.

I want to rest my head
against yours, let the soft
strength of your small hands
work the back of my neck and shoulders,

but you are nudging me back
saying it's only human
no one's strength
lasts forever.

Of such a single courage,
peaceful and whole,
I want to thank you for your caring
these years I've lived away.

In your respose
I see the roads I've chosen
are more traveled than narrow,
more embraced than abandoned,

no matter the headwinds
buffeting one's direction,
quagmires and potholes
stumbles and starts

gravelling my windshield.
This is my road grown out of yours,
the way paved with intention,
tempered with warmth and dimension.

MASTECTOMY, THE MOON

The moon seems
abstract to her,

like an x-ray of her breast.
Strange, she thinks,

the endless void
of space

packed with stars,
a thin moon

no more than
a tissue specimen,

slice of her sopped life
under a slide,

hanging there
for all to see

or not…
a severe thing,

severed, the
less than wholesome

wholeness
of her former self

on display,
radiating its malice.

ENVISION

I

After the doctor calls to tell you
your mother's suffered a catastrophic
at-the base-of-the-brain, main-stem stroke,
that she is conscious but paralyzed
from the neck down, that she can neither talk
nor swallow, that her vital functions are fading,
that she will be given no oxygen,
food, water, only saline, but made
comfortable and as the dying process
bears down on her morphine
will ease her pain, to let her rest
between each breath
as her breathing's sure to become labored.

—What is it you imagine of her last moments
lying there, unable to cry out,
to respond with only the blinking of an eye
to questions from family members
concerned with her comfort, the priest
administering last rites, a sister
placing my phone call from Missoula
to Flint, Michigan, up to her ear
so that I might offer words of comfort,
my love, news of her granddaughter Karin,
home from Alaska with her boyfriend Sean,
who've been away a full year working,
whom she last saw when still a child.

II

—What is it you envision with perhaps
a stroke someday of your own
with nothing so much as a blinding
bewilderment helping you cope
with your helplessness, while the animal-body
part of you, broken down, begins
its awkward but sure passage back

to humus, mineral in soil, where
your one good eye closes then opens
to a blur of faces praying you see
and remember them but can't be sure
what the slight tremors in a corner
of your mouth might mean,
or what sense if any to make
of the sounds coming from your throat—
so unfamiliar that not even you
can dream them intelligible,
anymore more than your physician
himself, with all his training, can.

—Except, later on, when
long past midnight, the family
having left quietly for a little rest
back home, your nurse, stethoscope
back on her shoulder, slowing folding
your hands in hers, your doctor
listening over your mouth,
a hand on your same forehead,
thumb and forefinger sweeping down
your descending gaze…how rarely
he verbalizes anymore but you're sure
he's thinking: life is, coming in,
life was, going out, all of it,
epic, a struggle for sure,
gracious even in its loss.

LETTER BACK TO MICHIGAN

"Eekelof Said there is a freshness
nothing can destroy us.
Not even we ourselves."
—John Logan

It is not memory alone that isolates
but vision arcing back now
urging me not to file away,
until another time,
a more convenient moment, —an answer
to your letter, your decision to scrap
a university's six-month
composition stint
for an honest machine-shop's wages,
a two-year contract to get your feet
back on the ground, and those half dozen
snapshots of self, son, expectant wife,
and on your lap in armchair,
your lop-eared, cock-eyed mutt—
how apt you dubbed him "Slump."

Remember the good years on the job,
the lit courses you loved to teach,
your university without notice dropping
the works flat, and you bolted,
traveling west for another crack
while wife held the kids, worked the hospital?
Months you knocked about hoping doors
might open something you might fill.
For months hadn't tenured department heads
on bond, thank you sorry, much regret,
positions filled, by all means keep in touch,
stacking your interest up, your response
turning hard then harder yet for glib,
officious, academic politic.

*

Years roll back now. We stood fine there—
our husky tile-shower voices booming,
our smoky clunkers floored, sandlot
one-on-ones, our spit-shined loafers,
our drive-in cuddlies cooing,
driving first real needs for love.
Something real, warmth and feeling
dates yearned for when our 'moving in'
instead came on too strong.

And didn't something new take hold
when death struck us both cold?
For me, my only father ever, gone,
dead at 50, his coarse graying hair
slicked back wrong, the deafening silence
his hands held a rosary in, the bastard
funeral director selling
flower arrangements
mother planned for friends,
hospitals, rest homes; you, your tall
all-cub kid brother, as sudden,
bike parts scattering a road,
wrapped in white ceremonial
burial cloth beside your heaving
and the body of parlor flowers
you aimed to break before you broke,
sat and wept.

*

Michigan. What was it drove me west?
You back? In this shot, your dog,
determined pup, tugs at length
on something…a tie, shred of hope perhaps?
—the other end of which, there at the margin,
does not itself let go. I know that pull
and sometimes picture it looped like rope
around my neck, the loop
tightening circles inside my head.

I often wonder if leaving home
might not have been the man but boy
running off toying with his grief.

I turn my back to the wall, pick up your letter,
settle again into your direct refreshing prose.
Looking out my window now…I see
fault block mountains, crusts of earth
thrust to dizzy height. I see ancient
glacial cirque, sheer saw tooth ledge,
then, drop rock down, sedge, fescue,
sorrel on foothills down. River bottoms next:
heron, whitetail, cottonwood, fox.
Snow you can touch all summer,
melts at timberline. Listen,
you'd think as things happen,
—scenery would be enough.

*

Montana. It was Michigan, Lansing,
then east where for kicks hours on end,
like kids, we made the most
out of a dismal day at the city dump.
Recall we didn't mope over indifferent graves
in rain but took to lengths of willow,
unraveled upholstery thread, dashboard knobs
for bobbers, hairpins wedged in car seats,
worms under rock and whatever else
we turned up turning back the clock.
And wasn't it our luck to catch
fish between us, a sunfish was it,
a bluegill, and stunning runts at that?
Big kids know just enough.

*

Here or there, we do what counts.
There is that choice. For family,
friends, we do what we can
hoping what we do is right.
For ourselves, don't we do much
growing wiser older?
So, when a camera brings us close
there is no choice. Images
lock us in, bring us home.
And here you are
tangling your danger in-between,
loaded grease gun at your head,
blueprint wadded in your mouth.
And here you are…
money mock-heroic,
cashing laughs in on the spot.

We frame ourselves and think
in the scene we're over-exposed.
There are stances taken in the nick of time,
when, whether by luck, fate, brain or brawn,
—whatever it is we are we become
in an instant, as thunderous clap,
humble, glad we've gone a little ape.
Can you see it, years from now,
photos under lamp shades fade
and we're up on that mountain top
we always talked about
(still looking for those caves in rock
the hum of silence comes from)
where, in an instant, a sudden pulse,
clouds dissolve, the sky breaks
—and words, words from everywhere
around the world, look straight at us

—and rave and rave?

II

ARCHETYPES

Fire comes. Infants of the region
of white wings, frightened of wings,

gather in small boats.
Fire comes. A woman knows the smoke.

The thunder of white wings!
The man withdraws, awed.

His breast-bone shakes.
Months later water breaks.

A small boat suffers through the smoke.
A man, a woman,

Their hour unfolding over earth,
stars mingling in their blood,

bear the rapture their living
flesh and bloods become.

They rest a little while,
blood, bone, and breath,

loving how hard it is they ache.

THE DEVIL AS A SECOND GRADER

(After working in the Poetry in the Schools program)

Can you guess what goes with it
when the tallest tree in the world,
falls down?

One said nests.
Another, birds.
This kid spelled it out: S K Y.
A few poked at clouds.
Many went far as Mars,
girls settling for the whitest stars.

Then somebody
in the back row
teacher seldom counts on
but when he's there
could growl
says
                God

    three times,

real loud.

THE REQUEST

Dear Friends:

Though it is itself
non-adhesive, that is,
the task, the proof
is to lick it
on the back of a stamp.

Lend the paste of it
to your word.

P.S

Now taste the provision
of a postcard.

—Send me some news.

SEAGULL

After Jonathan Livingston

Now as the earth
exposed its gentle neck
and surf licked up
photographic sand
and mussels
peaked in the flood,
as bell-throated buoys
pushed traffic past
and lanterns
joined the brassy moon,
—I held my breath.

O poets of great caprice,
hear me!
This is where
those long songs end.
Lo, the vision mounts,
swoops, stoops,
is stepped on and stumped.
It struts through sand like a fish.

HORSE IN THE BARN, CAT IN THE LOFT, PUDDLES ON THE FLOOR, BARD AT HIS BATH

I am naked, stripped before you,
your bar of Brambleberry soap,
slip off your rings, sweet thing,
dive at me like a cormorant.
Tackle my legs the way a cat rubs.

There. Now I'm Mark Anthony,
covered with suds and sturdy.
Say, things are out of hand,
fetch that kettle of water,
this soap's in a pickle,
getting kind of surly.

By gum, you've got some class,
that was a blast, you're a hoot,
now you're going to drop me
like an old boot? Pony up there, filly,
whilst I mosey around the tub
getting a grip on my captivity,
stretching things a bit.
I have plans Egyptian cliff-hanger.
I know the ropes.

THE DANCE

You're at this party and final
next to the prettiest girl there,
what will you do? Dash a cigarette
in your shoe? Pick a number
from one to ten, decide innocence
is a good disguise, rise
like a swan in a trance
and ask her to dance. And what'll

she do in your wings, fling herself
famous and fair, beat you to breakfast,
think you handsome, quiet by cool,
in your lofty common sense,
a cinch? Nothing to lose
and why not she sighs, the things
girls do if you just give them an inch.

GALLERY

I

Because I'm 'husky'
I lend a hand
setting an aluminum ladder up
a local
newspaper lady needs
to adjust ceiling lights
for right exposure
so, the Gallery Director
can pose with the artist
by an abstract oil for a photo.

"People don't go for pictures
unless they're full of people,"
her Polaroid snaps. "You two
plus a caption'll ice it,
get you gobs of visits."

Later I hear
the director ask
another class of kids
on a field trip,
what they think expression
with a breath of fresh air is.

II

Annex Room Two hosts an exhibit
entitled Earth Busts,
a voluminous study in clay
of exquisitely sculptured breasts
spirited deepest plum, honey spun,
blazing bright nipples.

One kid, adventuresome, the
Director's back turned,
licked a good one, yum.
Gee friends giggled milling about.

Whoa! I said to myself,
the footing on my composure
getting slippery,
rash tones
developing on my surface now
like a cheap photograph.

No purchase like your own
pinched yearnings, tethered pony,
gumming bits of propriety,
—the newspaper lady winks back.

RAMBLIN' ON THE WAY TO WALLACE, IDAHO

(Once famed for its glorious whore houses)

Pray for him
he's driving interstate 90,
his fun's getting hard to manage.
Days ago, only sage brush
licked him back off the road.
Approaching the Rest Stop,
he gears down, mumbling,
fumbling for a seedy love.
On page twelve a lady tumbles,
in Navy woolens
buttocks boiling in a spree,
his thumbs turning purple
on the wheel. He lurches
over a speed bump
to the moon on twenty.
Beams of lunar waters
gleam on supple summery buttered thighs.
His breath jolts hot and dry.
Inch by alluring inch, "Sasha" unfolds
her withing centerfold form
on pages twenty-two and three,
nerve goose-bumped
right up to her chin,
her brazen tongue
dabbling around inside
a wild inviting, mouth.
She's burning, begging him
to spend on her
his great pockets from behind.
"Sasha" turns his rig savage,
a macho rocket spilling stars.
She lights his dash alive.
Blood idles inside his brain.
Her man! He jerks
upright in his seat, scrapping the script,
stomping on the throttle,

launching his freight,
his high-wheeling, chrome-crowned,
evil, leather-padded, flag flying
self-possessed, resolute,
double-clutching 18-wheeler diesel,
tooting…thudding down the road!

A CULT OF SALT

Mary.
that night
we raged,
wild, savage,
goat-gloved, drunk.
We wanted the moon
brutal gentler.
We drank it empty and flat.

That night we raged,
sour-gutted,
fist-faced,
dead certain
we'd scraped away the past
and scratch up stars.

Remember?
We crept apart
and wakened strangers.
We knocked on
knot-wormed wood.
We bolted walls up tight.

Mary.
That dark
night-nest
seven-dollar slot
we sought
wasn't ample,
but a rash chance
in a cult of salt.

LINES FROM MY PENCIL

I feel like the bitter end.
The honey in this hive is ample green.
Bees pick on my watch.
A home's made of good skin.

My sensitive end's a tip-off.
A corkscrew on the bottle,
I go up my pipe like smoke.
This is a boat, our breath
in a sail, air under water.

Remember that day? It's all
in the dark. So I blacked out,
slapdash, up your skirt to my hip?
Listen: skin is for keeps…
The sky lit up like a match.

You're back. It's been tough
jumping off the top of my head.
Oh, I've had it with good behavior,
the deep end. Let's put it this way:
back in the saddle, high in the heart.

SALT AGAINST YOUR NAME

> *"We're strapped for cash. Ken's
> had to sell our seventh home
> to pay the bills."*
> —Enron's Ken Lay's wife

Day's tumble domino in windy seas,
rigging going slack, bows coming 'round,
canvas sails snapping full, bronze suns
accentuating cheek bones.

Economies on shore
float on junk bonds
floating on
leveraged pyramids of debt.

CEOs fidget in hearings,
loft verbal carnations
intimating white-collar coffers
never gifted trustees or their crones.

Gravity flows downhill,
public as a ditch.
Clear cut whitewash
soaks up a company's books.

In a vacating parking lots
milkweeds dry, splits on stalks.
Something in this bubble
cues a seedy spume.

In a chamber of your heart
modest songs decompose.
The world washes out
under your feet,

your beach slopped with spoils.
Your cunning peters out.
Clutch all the straw you need.
Greed can drag a man downhill.

WORDS I LIIKE TO HEAR

I'm putting on a show in my shoe.
I'm laced right to my kisser.
I'm not bowing out in the cold.
I'm stepping ahead into my exit.

What's going on on the cob?
I have an image at hand
with butter on my chine.
I'm green inside all this music.

Who can say of our meals,
right here on top of our toast,
—we're not satisfied with our bones?
Mama, my blood runs when you're home.

Razzle-dazzle, I'm coming unglued?
You say it's cold when I know?
I say I'm buttoned up to here.
I make tracks when it snows.

SESTINA POLITTI

(Re: G.W. Bush)

Call it amazing
how a small head of state
stumbles among daffodils
sans imagination, born
with a film of oil in his mouth greasing the loop
in his mind denying all but the chosen any kind of hope.

You'd think with a little hope
amazing
things might happen, momentum for instance a loop
unfurls at the crack of a whip. Functionaries of state,
however, hinging on this and that being borne
away in committees, nod off like daffodils.

The stems of daffodils
can be carved into flutes so hope,
rinsed with assuring notes, soaks up stillborn
thought, but complicities as amazing
as ever rise from cups of state
only to evaporate like steam in a loop.

One feels so lost in the misty loop
of it all. Beyond daffodils,
dazed like apologists in a state
of disgrace, the faithful soar for hope
from pop star to born-again dolts. Amazingly
they fall for revivals, pomp, wind-born

ceremonies, patently lavish. But born
to a challenge, consensus jells and the tasteful loop
between truth and imagination is amazing.
We pick with our teeth daffodils
if we have to, and hope
to hell our heartless proponents of state

have backbone enough to state
the obvious—how our fear of them is borne
by the homeless, how surplus could mean hope
for the poor, a word like "Welcome" loop
light over any town flattened in the dark. Teething on daffodils
they ape it up ornamental lawns, amazing.

Soup lines of reality are amazing.
This side of the truth, daffodils connect:
one world, one need, one pulse, one loop.

III

PASTORAL ON A CORK CLIPBOARD

Cellulose with format.
Wedded syllables whorled by sea wind.
White caps on a blue shoal, foam slips.
Cry of plover, turnstone, tern,
pop of kelp pods where we step,
our ears ringing.

Kids are butterflying sand mounds,
up oak-leafed trunks they breeze,
limb after limb becoming freckle-kissed,
cricket lipped. Dew beads on weed stems
spin an early summer sheen,
green glaze. Lush straw basket,
French bread crust,
wine glasses, cheddar wedge.

Aloft in port haze, lazy ship smoke.
An elemental breeze
in madrone leaves, sweet shade,
-our blanket down. Salt
of pimento, pastrami, baked gold
of egg white. Among flower-petals
whirs like small ten-speeds,
copper-red iridescences,
trick aircraft principally,
maneuvering nature-patented invisibilities,
—Hummingbirds!

Absolute radiance without issue,
the pulse of things, their sheer sense.
All our moorings before us,
—it is not without expectation
our flesh stirs, grateful
our hand in hand world,
everything here making us
if only for the moment
so much larger for where we are
lifting our eyes to clarity, clear as wine.

LAND DEVELOPERS WALKING INTO A FIELD

A kid Schwinns a hill,
his dad's proud
balloon-tire restoration
spinning up a casual wind
fluttering through
his yellow sleeves.
In the distance, ravens' squabble.
Closer, cattle rattle corns stalks
mooing over cobs tumbling into root troughs.

Muskrats splash in cattails.
Where pavement puddles to a crossroad,
swells, rises into the next hill,
he waves to a woman pulling carrots.
The honest motions his legs make
churns the sprocket. Layered
in a matrix, engineered just so,
the asphalt glides over dips and vales
in the earth like a hand does
in a doeskin glove teasing out folds in a robe.

She checks her shoes at the door,
lifts her apron up into the sink,
gathers a smile pulling back her hair.
Last December, straight from storage,
carrots and yams, potatoes,
a bottle of her own elderberry wine
graced a hickory-smoked Christmas ham.

This poem does not explain who they are,
where they live, if they know each other
or how the day for them might
or might not be inextricably mixed.
There's not much of an attempt either,
to write an irascible pheasant off,
tawny-chested, indigo sheen,
scarlet wattle, white neck ring,
iridescent green-black head
scattering sunlight through the corn.

He lacks a certain sophistication
once disturbed and his squawking
is something awful. Short
of skimming his topsoil off,
nothing can drive him away.
He rasps his one explicative
because what he's got, soon
to be cropped, chopped, tilled
into magnificent heaps
of manure and dirt…
is profit enough, for one day.

OUTSIDE DETROIT, DEEP IN THE 'BURBS

Pop's house, understand, is secure
but out of place, —old eraser-pink brick
smack in the middle of trendy
Green Briar Hills Development where I jog
in sweltering back-home Michigan heat
hoping to melt my middle-aged, class-reunioned,
party-soaked body back into some semblance
of my thirty-plus year ago, gridiron prep
ripple-suave, bonehead, ramrod shape.

Whereas neighbors reflect on flowers in plots
of aromatic bark, he cultivates a weedy yard
of clunkers for their sundry parts.
Each beams with scars from the Motor City's
hell-bent kingdom-come, rush-hour war,
—an odd epiphany of dings and nicks,
flakes of chrome peeling off
like so much sun burnt skin,

Here a trunk lid's sprung, a tire flat,
there, random chops to the body, in addition to,
one might say, new wrinkles in the way
fenders dent. He steps outside onto his porch,
crosses himself as if with Holy Water,
looks north, or is it south? Beats me,
I'm lost myself by now…his eyes

sweeping skyward imploring the gods
up there to make things go right, no matter what.
Far from the bridled gut of the upper
class itself, flesh sings above his belt
through a thinned out, washed up,
I'd put my money on a K-Mart
Blue Light Special summer shirt.

A fallen angel, displaced auto worker,
maybe bankrupt lotto winner, fat chance!
But surely a mother's dimpled son
if not foggy image of the very old

man himself, tries to reverse his fate
after having moved back home, —I imagine,
to take the slack out of his goosy life,
in these too well-groomed haughty country 'Burbs.

Plodding past him on my circuit,
I see him holding fast to footholds
of land his family once tenant-farmed,
out-flanked now by an avalanche of asphalt,
sporty rigs parked out front cookie-cutter
condos, where automatic timers
water uniform lawns without hedgerows,
clothes lines or fences, unleashed pets,
or freckled kids humming among dandelions
topped with insects. Head out a window,

neck craned, arm flattened against his door,
—there's not a chance he'll back down
against another spectacular, attractively
homogenous, celebrity launched,
community tax-draining, Factory Outlet Emporium.
Thus, he backs down his drive, then up the street
in reverse, through billowing plumes
of blue-grey smoke, when, damned
if he doesn't, pour on the octane,
rev up the rpms, the whole shebang
exploding in a screeching triumph
over a slick developer's zeal for vast cement.
Like that, —he slips around a barricaded corner,

flooring it backwards out of sight.

COLUMBUS, GEORGIA

*While passing through the deep south on our way
to Fort Lauderdale, Florida, swinging into
Fort Benning to pick up a friend soon to be
deployed to Vietnam, circa 1959.*

Picture a Black man sitting on a bench,
straps of his denim coveralls sliding
his shoulders, sweatband-stained hat
in his lap, head slumping in restful posture,

any strength sapped already in early morning
sticky southern heat. "Welcome," a billboard
boasts, toasting the town of Columbus, Georgia.
Stick 'em up, one of us blurts, laughing.

Not so fast, a local constabulary's siren fumes
seconds later, pulling us over, obnoxious flashing
throwing sand in our exhausted eyes, headlights
high-beamed on our Michigan plates.

A second patrol shows, batons soon
spreading our feet, hands flattened on roof top,
hood, our five wallets confiscated: Georgia's infamous
lawful highway men sizing up illegal dividends.

See the sign? City limit's 25 mph, a cop says.
We tripped up coasting in a little over thirty.
Traffic court's in session this afternoon,
another informs. You can pay the $100 fine

right now and be on your way. Split five ways,
not bad, we nod in unison. Instead, the greedy
fuckers pull $100 each from our wallets,
grinning, rich with conspiratorial cordiality.

See that fellow yonder on the bench?
Got it in his head once to quit the hog plant,
the throat-slitting, find another way
to make a living. Owner takes it unkindly,

prompts local toughs to re-arrange
that uppity boy's way of thinking.
Now look at him. Ironical, ain't it…
thinking he's so smart, can do what he wants.

You boys paying attention? Wouldn't
do right you-all returning to your mommas
looking like that. (The man's left eye
dangled from its socket, its ropy sleeve

of skin swinging like a bell-cord
when he turns his head.) Preacher says,
can't hurt 'em. God made 'em strong like ox,
meant for them to burden. Besides,

heaven's mysterious: judge says
a kid takes a lickin' just proves
he had it coming. Now he sits,
just laze around all-the-day.

Lord, you'd think he'd have gotten
that thing fixed by now.
No self-respecting white folk
gonna slink around town like that.

T'arnation, if he ain't an eyesore.

FINDING SOME TRACTION

There's a heavy, wet, end-of-May
snowstorm pestering town today
stalling bike and vehicle traffic,
and though I have cash
to slosh downtown for beer,
a spirited game of pool,
I'm feeling homebound,
yet hardly out of focus.
I'm sitting at my desk
peering through the reverse end
of a clunky pair of binoculars,
the lenses of which I've just dusted off.
At first glance a darkening tunnel,
my eyes adjusting to faint
concentric rings of light
then over the edge of what must be
part of the prism, then back
to more rings, they finally
tumble out into my coffee cup.
Far-off light from a reading lamp
floods the Kelly-green lettering
of a nearby soup can clutch
of #2H pencils. Brassy gizmos
securing rubber erasers in place,
gleam as well. A yellow notepad
plies the scene
across my well-grained
desktop slab of Tennessee red oak.
With the binoculars
still in place, I'm reading back
through stuff I've written down,
left to right, two, three words at a time
(you ought to try it)
looking for this and that
and I beg you to bear with me for a moment
while I try not to succumb
to the temptation to make
anything more of this casual event
I already have and leave it at that.

SURVIVING BIG-BONED DOMESTIC CHALLENGES IN THE WILDERNESS

In the back of his mind there's a father's concern
for his daughter, that if he isn't able
to get back in time, that she'd have to undergo
surgery on her own. He's booked, winter
float dates locked in and if he doesn't go
he loses them. He's worried about storms,
raging head winds slowing him down,
causing him to miss the pre-arranged
pick-up shuttle, or worst of all,
to find himself somehow flipped over,
stranded, out of reach, with only
the barest of provisions scooped from
the current, picked off sandbars,
raft and oars long swept from sight,
deep in the rugged, unbelievably beautiful,
magnificently indifferent, Grand Canyon.

Here's the scene: he's shying from friends
getting wind of his longing flowing under him.
He doesn't want the facts misconstrued,
that his permit to float the Colorado River
in his own raft, is a coveted, once in a lifetime
opportunity to do something special, to meet
the stiffest of challenges head on.
He admired the tenacity, raw courage,
astute observations of John Wesley Powell,
first American to float the river
in 1869, rowing, as best he could,
with a single arm, having lost the other
in the Civil War. He recalls
latter day giant of the southwest
Edward Abbey, in his book, *Desert Solitaire,*
bemoaning striking formations,
verdant side canyons, copious pictographs
in the not-too-distant future flooding over,
buried under silt and sand as the waters
back up behind a new Hoover Dam.
He had to know if he had to, he could be

like Powell, like Abbey. A man of action
himself, he liked that they slacked their thirst
straight up, by the cup, right from the river.
He couldn't wait to follow suit.

He's talked it over with his daughter,
got her to see his point of view,
that it'd be a shame not to take advantage
of such good fortune. What about hers?
What about others around him questioning
his motives? Was he committed enough
to get them to see things his way?
Hadn't many of them question
whether he'd intentionally, if ever,
accidentally abandon his daughter?
There's no way such a thing could happen,
because, if he had to, he'd swim, hike,
float his way back to the landing.
But it's a given, isn't it, people giving up,
siding with caution, failure to challenge
their limits? Isn't it about strengthening
one's character, adding muscle
to one's will? He wasn't the type
to let a little confusion get in his way.
Look, he said to himself. Weren't
contingency plans arranged earlier
at the Mayo Clinic? And wasn't it
part of an agreement to settle for
adventures of lesser proportions,
anyway? Well, whatever, he said to himself.

So a piece of cake the moment became
for his daughter, mother settling
out of state after the divorce.
She'll stand true to form, back
to a solid chip off her father's hard rowing,
muscle bound shoulders. "*Killer rapids?
Swamping boulders? Dicey-peachy!
No sweat! Bring 'em on!*" He says, taunting his fate.

Damn, but his machismo bugs her. What if
the raft's punctured, pulled under?
Who'd be around this time of year
to help him? If he had to, how'd he ever
climb his way out of that canyon?
And more than any of this, what if
complications set in once her spleen's
removed? And wasn't lupus
affecting her lungs? (*Systemic Lupus,
a chronic autoimmune disease
where one's immune system
treats a body's tissues
like a foreign substance.*)
Might that not have a bearing
on how well she shakes off anesthesia?
Here then, on her own two feet
she'll stand waiting for the biopsies
of her liver, lymph nodes.
Tough as nails, he prides himself,
the kid's a real trooper.

People again. Damn them.
Why can't they just bugger off,
as the Brits say? Oh, he can
hear them blathering: "Hey,
you're back, have a good time?"
And his rude neighbor, down the block,
licking his chops, getting his digs in—is sure to say:
"Look, you ducked out of the ballpark, man,
when you should have been up at the plate."

In this world one struggles with critics,
detractors, what they contend.
That's the price you pay rising above them.
They'd soon as dump a load
of crap at his feet setting his daughter
and himself apart. But their stuff

stinks. Fact is, flesh, blood, and bone,
he'll be home before anyone knows it.
Fact is, he's been journaling, practicing
the craft that'll tell all, admit
his misgivings even. He's determined
his feat will outlive its critics. Friends,
others, must learn to let things pass,
to know directly what is about
to take place, will do so
for no other reason than the love
he and his daughter have for one another.
Rest assured, when the dust settles,
when the measure of his achievement
is acknowledged, when the courage
with which his very daughter faced
her own wilderness of uncertainties,
her health triumphantly restored,
well, the public we know, won't they?

But given a massive canyon's
copious layers of crumbling rock...
gloriously crimson in their descending
sunset staircase air, and given such
a long-sought-after adventure,
monumental in its proportions,
humble in its conclusion,
well, who's to say the mighty Colorado
couldn't be tamed by a dude like himself
from good ol' Podunk Missoula, Montana, eh?

Jena Lindsay, his daughter, that's who.
Who, in childhood was his **missy freckle,
tickly potato,** (who, gathered up as she grew
more likenesses of mother than father)
who bonded to then rebounded from
the feckless nature of her parent's
relationships, their increasing eccentricities.
That something fundamental making
modest marriages work seemed missing.

It was as if, as French writer Albert Camus
spoke to in *The Rebel*, his grand essay
on the nature of man in revolt—that
certain emotional dilemmas lacked resolve,
*could not bear the cold implacable
clarity one must endure in order to live.*
Their commitment was now on the rocks
and they knew it. Exotic travel, though,
suggested fulfillment, authenticity
of a sort one only earns on his or her own.

But not for Jena Lindsay, for whom recovery
from surgery had slowed to incremental
compounded by post-operative depression,
joblessness, ballooning medical debt,
incompletes piling up, then with her boyfriend
Ian, unspecified troubles of his own brewing,
her despair suddenly unremitting
in the wake of his sudden bowing out…

—left Jena with nowhere to turn,
left her writing, "I'm sorry," on a
scrap of paper, who rose from her
kitchen table to empty a vase
of spent flowers Ian had given her
only a week ago, who drew tight
her kitchen curtains, her phone line
disconnected, strewn in a corner,
who didn't think twice about
blowing out her stove's pilot light,
who gulped some of a remaining prescription,

—her mooring's tearing loose,
pitching her overboard, adrift…
her will clouding over,
her cell phone jingling in the study
where she'd forgotten she'd
left it, sending her flying, not exactly
in a snit, as once imagined, but knowing,

as her phone rang and rang,
only Ian could be so faultlessly
devoted, and he was!

JIM AND THE THREE BEARS

Ten or so miles downstream
from the Giles Bridge
on the upper most part
of the famous blue ribbon trout stream
that Rock Creek is, my friend, Jim Heide,
stands, enjoying a wondrous day fishing.

In work-a-day tennies and paint splattered
cutoffs, he wades his way upstream
fishing deeper runs, boulder pockets,
a log jam or two, good water,
from one side of the Rock to the other,
the old creek living up to its fine reputation.

As juvenile rascals chased his flies,
white fish roll their sides, flashing silver,
his hand-tied Adams Irresistibles,
turkey-winged hoppers, elk-hair humpies,
floating up-right, riding native,
exactly overhead, high and dry.

He's crimped his barbs down
making releasing fish easier, easier on him,
same for his quarry. In his creel,
lined with field horsetail and mint,
his first keeper, a breakfast Rainbow,
rests on its wild bedding.

Finally hooking into a lunker,
a lunging five pounder, his fly rod bending
to its strength and heft, the fish
charges downstream flattening itself
against the current, his old banged up
Pflueger Medalist fly reel holding on,

fly line burning into its backing.
He's looking for witnesses, others on the water
who might corroborate his trophy

if he ever lands it. No such luck.
The fish, reverses direction,
plows its way back upstream, kicking up

a daisy chain of jumps and splashes
Jim's sure will catch the attention
of a trio of black bears, a momma
and her cubs, at just that moment,
crossing over to his side of the Rock.
What to do? Already in a corner,

he backs into another, a pocket on the bottom
he can squat in, sink in up to his chin.
He's hidden, he assures himself
as he backs deeper into the shade
bank bush offers. As he exhales
strings of bubbles leak in the current.

Meanwhile, his pencil-thin flyrod,
still in a tumultuous tug-a-war with the fish,
keeps changing directions like a whip lash,
and he knows it'll give his position away.
Sure enough, the cubs spot Jim first, skid to a stop,
momma bear then abruptly plowing into both.

The three of them now, a mere 10 feet away,
are watching: Jim first, then his fish,
then back to Jim, all the while momma bear
growing impatient, growls, cuffs a cub,
all three then heading downstream in a huff,
gone in seconds. Jim regains his composure,

thanks the current for rinsing out his shorts.
Vowing to keep his folly secret, what else
can he do but rein in his fish, thank it, kiss it goodbye,
let it go. He crawls up the bank, finds a dry spot,
a stump to sit on. He loosens his laces, shakes
gravel out of his shoes, looks around,

—digs a pocket for a soggy cigarette.

WATER TO SUSTAIN THE SPIRIT

I've found for myself a place
that gives thought
to small scale management.
A deepening sense
of things, one within another,

fills the moment.
The flow's resplendent
and each thing fits.
It gives me pause,
enough to know

I could just as well dally on the surface,
contentedly dependent,
little more than cork in a current,
my days skipping by like stones.
The task is not to stub this old toe,

so I'm unwinding on a gravel bar
populated with sandpipers, wild scent.
I'm at large here, home.
There's a steady ovation on my side,
a white-water riffle racing west.

I see how plant roots hold
a river's soils down, how grasses
and sedges diminish silting
and on riverbed gravels
algae grow where aquatic insects feed

and trout slash currents
slapping their tails in the sun.
A heron rookery battens down
a stand of cottonwoods,
gnarled limbs bleached with droppings.

Nesting cavities are opening
and canopies will soon fill with song.
Once I would have cut a path
so carts of firewood from dying
or broken might keep me warm.

It's quieter now watching squirrels
and jays, white-tailed deer,
warblers spilling out of thickets,
wasps constructing paper domes.
A pail of morels in spring,

summer berries by the cup,
my creel lined with field horsetail
and mint, a wild West Slope Cutthroat Trout,
—are benedictions, each and all,
unbroken promises of the earth.

Distinctions, landscapes,
sky, island, slough,
eagles under cumulus, swallows
nesting cutbanks, beaver, coyote, weasel,
dragonflies lifting from water's edge,

their cellophane-like wings
igniting in the sun—
I hold and behold the world.
It is here, there. Everywhere part of me.
I take it with me when I go.

IV

JASPER IN SUNSHINE

With respect to Walt Whiteman and Carl Sagan

I

October chills in the shade.
Our star flares deep in space.
The sun's glare
storms through windows
enclosing our front porch.
It's my umpteenth year
on planet Earth
and I'm open more than ever
to such floods
of shameless sunlight.
The funnel end of vastness
pouring in, I'm awash in a sea
of photons, their wild
cosmic warmth
keeping the little chemistries
of my skin afloat.

I sort through collections
of crystals, mineral specimens
our retirement years
are digging up for us.
We display them
for the enjoyment of others,
friends and neighbors
awaiting our welcome at the door:
smoky quartz from Lolo Pass,
amethysts for jewelers
from Crystal Park,
swirling metamorphic rock
from the Lochsa River
in Idaho. A translucent
half-inch thick shard
of evaporate gypsum,
laid down by ancient inland seas
millions of years ago,

scattered every which way
like broken plate glass—
unexpected obstacles
my son and I once crawled across
putting the sneak on antelope
feeding on a far hill
near Roy, Montana, years ago…

II

Here's some plain mudstone,
(wind or water-rippled, roadcut common)
laid down during a young planet's
formatively long, oxygen absent,
Precambrian era, where
at just the right moment
in deep time,
primitive algae first grabbed hold
of the physics of quantum mechanics,
converting the solar energy of photons
into the chemical energy
of vegetative growth.
In the process, carbon dioxide
broke down, locked carbon up,
released oxygen. Oxygen,
molecules beyond number,
enlivened earth's once suffocating
nascent air shed. Photosynthesis,
established, started connecting
all the dots, became a new library
of earth's reality and everyhere
chlorophyll raged, life took instruction
and the planet greened up.

III

Take this slip of jasper,
a gift my geology friend, Bruce Cox,
dug up summers ago
somewhere in Wyoming.
Lifting it into the sun,
its blood richness deepens in the sun.
I imagine billions of photons
streaming off its surface,
in all their fizzy brightness
clouds of them alighting
on random dust motes,
amusing the hairs of my arms,
setting up camp on the tips
of my eyelashes. Listen,
who hasn't placed a straw hat
over his or her head
for the fun of it,
for the sake of going about
one's business, safely of course,
just to marvel at the performance
of the sun's rays
flickering through golden oat fields
meshed in the weave of an old hat?
Imagine the view
inside such a cloud chamber
of possibilities, lighting up an old muse,
coaxing him into discovery.

IV

My hat's off to this microcrystalline
variety of quartz. In the same family
as moss agate and banded onyx,
jasper is beautiful in its own way
and for now, it owns me.

If I were to say
at this stage of my life
I've become involved
over a pile of rocks,
you'd be right.
The strain of living a good life
in times of public strife,
where a once essentially descent nation,
is now made a mockery of,
leaves us little choice
but plant our feet,
pursue what small pleasures
we can despite our country's
belligerent leadership,
entitlements of the wealthy,
its corrosive politics.
We're grounded survivors,
healthier for our treks
to various deposits.
And it's not just the rocks
capturing our attention.
Flora and fauna
flesh out our visits as well.
We're enriched, proud
to be informed,
open to new pursuits
and directions.
We love our collections,
the stories they hold.
We're convinced
it's not a bad way to grow old.

V

Two hundred years ago
Walt Whitman began singing
his body electric. Celebrating himself,
he loafed and invited his soul

observing a spear of summer grass.
He reminded us that every atom in me
as good belongs to you. Further along,
he asked whether we had pride enough
to get at the meaning of poems.
And he knew without saying
matter hasn't a soul without us.
Might this have been what Whitman,
ahead of his time, put his finger on
without knowing it?

When the late astrophysicist
Carl Sagan exclaimed:
"We are the stuff of stars
matter become conscious,"
he too sweetens our glimpse
as to how things evolve,
work on the deepest levels.

Extending the metaphor,
magnifying our optics,
our overview of the cosmos,
our place within it,
what could be more humbling
than the idea of a selfless nature
reinventing itself over and over
through the lives of its stars,
super novia, its elements,
its life forms, a continual
resupplying of all needed
to keep going in perpetuity?

VI

I want to understand how atoms
of silica and oxygen link up,
one complex lattice
after another, stacked

as only their chemistries allow,
the resulting mix—
a hard and durable mineral.
Imagine for a moment
other such star-generated
riches resting on your palm:
might it be cubic, hexagonal,
dendritic, kidney-shaped, massive,
rhombic, conchoidal, terminate,
greasy, opaque, silky, or translucent?
Is it flakey like mica or a fool's tale?
Does it glisten, flare in the eye
like fire-opal does when turned it light?

Oh, there's so much to go around.
Look: the path to our porch is concrete enough.
Pun aside, good as gold, we applaud,
again and again, what nature spells out for us.

John Holbrook lives with wife Judith in Missoula, Montana, where he earned his masters degree in Creative Writing from the University of Montana. In 1990 his poem "Petition to Common Sense," won first place in the Florida Poetry Contest, juried by the poet and Novelist, James Dickey. In 1991, his first book, *Clear Water on the Swan*, shared first place with short story "Writer," Ron Fischer, in Montana Arts Council's First Book Award. In 2002 Pudding House Publications published his chapbook, *Loose Wool, river Tackle, Pencil Drafts*, a manuscript which grew out of a grant from the Ludvig Vogelstein Foundation to write a sequence of poems on various rivers in his region. In 2010 Foothills Publishing of Kanona, New York, published his collection *A Clear Blue Sky in Royal Oak*. Over the years his work has appeared nation wide in many magazines and periodicals including *Antaeus; Barataria review; Big Sky Journal; Cafeteria; Camas, The Carolina Quarterly, Colorado State review; Comstock Review; Cutbank; The Florida Review; Fresh Water Poems* (an anthology); *Of Frogs and Toads* (an anthology); *Green Hills Literary Review; Hubbub; Kinesis, Main Street Rag; Mississippi Review; The Nebraska Review; The New Verse News; Pinyon; Poetry Northwest; Rain City Review; The South Carolina Review; Southern Poetry Review; The Talking River Review* and the *Wisconsin Review*, to name a few.

www.ingramcontent.com/pod-product-compliance
Lightning Source LLC
Chambersburg PA
CBHW030059170426
43197CB00010B/1590